Trusting the I

PEGGY POOLE

Brentham Press

First published 1994 by
Brentham Press 40 Oswald Road, St Albans, Herts AL1 3AQ

ISBN 0 905772 44 X

British Library Cataloguing-in-Publication Data
A catalogue record for this book is available from the British Library

Printed in England by Intype London SW19 8DR

for Mary, with love and admiration

also by Peggy Poole

Poetry
Never a put-up Job
Cherry Stones and Other Poems
No Wilderness in Them
Midnight Walk
Hesitations

Children's Fiction (as Terry Roche)
Brum
Shadows on the Road
Your Turn to Put the Light Out

Adult Fiction (as Terry Roche)
Sprig of Wild Heather

Contents

Acknowledgments
For poems previously published or broadcast acknowledgment is due
to:- Acumen, Aireings, Beehive Press, BBC North, BBC Radio
Merseyside, Eastern Rainbow, Envoi, Envoi Summer Anthology 1991,
Iota, Iron, Lace Prizewinners, Lancaster Literature Festival 1991 and
1992, Outposts, Phoenix Press, Vision On.

SENSING PERIMETERS

The tenth step from the cliff edge
silences
estuary music;
I can no longer hear
sea conversation
with the shore.
Eyes only are allowed
such healing power.

Sight permits renewal
from that ebbing, flowing
to partner grace of grasses,
flowers and trees;
but the broad back of land
commands selection,
choice between bird-song
and shift of sand.

I count the steps
that take me from sea voices,
weave back and forth to make
my wishes clear
and wonder what other secrets
earth denies me,
what other sounds
I am not yet allowed to hear.

SYMBIOSIS

Life beside this river tells
that nothing can remain the same;
sand shifts in turning days, and rocks
brandish knives or hide submerged;
estuaries threaten or beguile.

Flowers and trees and grasses dance
in a rhythmic ritual:
trunk gain only slowly shows,
leaves linger, blossoms cling
but time and change mark everything.

In the song of land and sea
in frost fever, summer balm,
each hill and valley, primrose, birch
offers grace, and ebbing tides
channel paths for our evolving.

SEA SPECTACULAR

I have seen phosphorescence, stood entranced
as waves broke into jewels one summer night
and fishermen cast turquoise leaves, hulls danced
on opal petals. Such a magic sight
I never thought to see so close at home
confining it to some Pacific bay
not on this unsung stretch where I come
in almost every weather, day after day.

Science can give explanations why
but when stars applauded, naiads played
that night on the water, I wanted to cry
in delight, in wonderment, but stayed
silent, eyes darting there and there
expecting a Christ-like figure to appear.

JELLYFISH

They populate the marine lake
                    this morning;
translucency adds lustre
                    to green weeds;
bodies rise and fall
                    as tutus
in a class of budding
                    ballerinas.

They almost make me forget
                    – these young ones –
my horror when swimming
                    of that sting
that revulsion when shore–walking
                    at slimy circles
left by the tide to wither
                    in the wind.

Staring at these creatures
                    of the ocean –
their scalloped bodies,
                    distinct markings –
I rejoice in such delicacy
                    and grace
link with the origins of life.

UNSEAWORTHY

At low tide
that small white hull
resting on the sand
appears inviting;
it seems to lie in wait
ready to take me beyond
familiar shores.

But the dinghy,
now the sea has flooded in,
is submerged,
only its rim peeps
above water.
It will never carry me,
never sail again.

Yet it comforts still:
holds dreams for children
who play near, brings
memories to adults; heron
will feed there in autumn.
Even holed, boats
fulfil a need.

FORCE 8

Warnings of gales came
when I was driving home to warmth.
The maroon gun propelled my cat
underneath the bed, made me run
to watch the lifeboat leap the waves
and pray for those in danger
– child, yachtsman, tourist
who's misjudged the tide –
and for the crew, friends who
over years have rescued strangers.

Closing curtains against spray–lashed glass,
I exclude weather, but all evening
wonder if distant searchers
battle still, not knowing
as they trough through cliffs of water
if this launch will be successful,
whether all will come home tonight.

I am one with those silent gatherings
at slipways, huddled against fear,
staring into mist, listening
for voices on the tide, tired
triumphant tones that tell of lives saved,
or, when the engine dies, a silent
coming in, wading ashore, Coxswain
slowly seeking one young wife
who reads the message in his eyes.

TELL'S TOWER

For years it stood alone
in the grounds of Hilbre House
that became the Speaker's home;
a monument to guide travellers
across miles of estuary
like the lighthouse at Talacre
on the opposing Celtic coast.

Erected over the grave
of a champion St Bernard
"noble and of undaunted courage"
the circular tower is now
part of a modern bungalow,
titillated with ruched curtains
and ripe pear carpets, struggling
to retain significance.

One April I had to call on Selwyn Lloyd
to apologise for a missed appointment
lying about being unwell
not wanting to admit slothful memory.
Standing among primroses and bluebells
in the tower's shelter, he confided
while picking me some flowers
his intention, on return to London,
to rule the phrase "a pack of lies"
as unparliamentary which in future
would be disallowed in the House of Commons.
Was he saying he saw through my excuses?

Rain and wind test the turret's
sandstone rising from red brick;
today, walking my dog on the shore,
I contemplate courage and truth.

HOLIDAY INSTRUCTION

You led me, brother mine, from milestone
to milestone on Cornish holidays:
persuaded me, aged four, early one morning
by the campfire near our tent
to welcome pepper on poached egg;
taught me to float in waters
round St Michael's Mount
and summer after summer took me
scrambling cloud high
above rocks white−foamed with waves
to find chough and cormorant.

I never confessed that each night
fear seized control, flung me
from anchoring clumps of grass
to those jagged jaws below;
the force of falling
would jerk me out of sleep.

No cliff−fall
but bullets killed you
when you were twenty−one. Yet still
you season my days, throw me
to depths, lift me
to unexplored heights.

WOUNDED

I need to be with water and alone
refill my empty vessel and atone;
I need to trek woodlands, talk with trees
climb hills and headlands, drink their peace;
allow sunsets to soothe my soul
let sea susurrations make me whole.

DESERT ISLAND DISCS

Forget the discs and desert. I will choose
the landscape of my island. Don't refuse
me heathered hills pointing to the sky,
with outcrops of rock and stones; may I
for survival find, high up, a spring
that trickles down with elemental song
to a waterfall above a lake, where trees
(willow, various fruits and elder, please)
will shade and solace. Let there be meadows
where daisies and poppies in grasses grow
with barley—corn between. When autumn comes
would it break the rules to ask for mushrooms?

Across these fields to the gaoler sea
twists a river like a lane. Give me
a ridge of firs if possible so that
at Christmas I've something to decorate.
Three yards at least no tide will ever touch
of honeyed sand that makes up the beach.
I'd like, if it's allowed, one more request:
a secret valley with a floor of moss.
Castaways may also have their choice
of one luxury. I want a lighthouse.
Which would be the most important of all
these requests? The spring on the purple hill.

HAIKU

Lone white butterfly
searching the shore, bewildered
to find no flowers.

LAST NIGHT OF THE ILLUMINATIONS

Hanging above our heads
garish tea—pots pour
glitter into sparkling cups.
Miss Muffet sits — but runs
repeatedly from that spider.

Humpty Dumpty falls
four times in one minute;
kings and queens and teddy bears
dance along the prom, while
from the Tower a laser scrawls the sky.

On this last Sunday evening
everything is open:
windows, funfairs, pubs, sex—shops,
mouths for chips, candyfloss and popcorn;
coaches and hotels spill people out.

As dawn breaks a bossy wind
chases debris into corners
and the sea sweeps in
to impose order on
this razzmatazz of a town.

HIS USUAL PINT
(for A.F.)

He always drank a pint of Castlemaine
when imbibing with a group of friends
in our local pub at each day's end.

Facing redundancy at forty-five
he would not let himself confess defeat,
rejoiced, some weeks on, when he could greet

them with news of another job.
He shared their interests and together
they groused about politics, prices, weather.

Came, then, the time they met in solemn mood
agreed to buy his usual pint to stand
beside their drinks as if to wait his hand;

It stood untasted while each one recalled
the previous evening's casual "Good-night"
and seemed to be a suitable salute.

PUDDLE

Bird—bath
puppy—drink
toddler—temptation
nuisance
for walkers
non—entity
with no
reflection

reflection
of sky
leaves
faces
a painting
photograph
sudden masterpiece
in a road

road
of tall
Victorian
terrace houses
one here caught
with me
in a puddle
this picture
excites
tarmac—framed

framed by rainfall
I long
to lift it
intact
carry it
to hang
on the white walls
of my hospital
room.

FLAG AT HALF MAST

Like the tolling bell
it is signal and salute
though who was first accorded
such a tribute is lost
in history's centuries.
Was it some
Celtic chieftain,
his body brought by barge
up-river for burial
or an early English queen
carried in court ceremonial?

Wind makes candle flame, burning
for a loved one, falter
but enlivens this homage.
The flag, before being lowered,,
is sent to the mast top
to celebrate a life
however briefly lived.
It is best suited
to grey skies, poignancy
overwhelms against a setting sun.

From city hall or village church
liner or lone yacht
unchanged in its message
whether flown for Nelson,
the seven lost in Challenger,
yesterday's politician,
a you or a me,
it meets death without a whine,
grants a gracious goodbye
and bestows on mourned and mourner
a touch of magic.

WREATHED IN WATER

She does not struggle, lies buoyed by her dress.
From her fingers float daisies, poppies;
dogroses are growing by the stream.
Weeds wait to receive her when she sinks,
reeds and crowfoot make their own farewell.
The ancient willow leans across to hear
strange songs of lamentation as she stares
at a patch of sky, seeks her father's face.
A witness later spoke of fusion with water;
there is mystery in the painting, in the pose.

Each suicide breeds questions
though none look tranquil like this;
when despair flings its minder off a bridge
the body, dragged from the river,
bears no flowers, holds no peace.

Young Millais thought it fitting
women should seek death for love
or grief for a father. His model's
patience in cold water must have
touched his heart. An overdose of laudanum
ended her brief life. Did his brush
not falter, did he not feel a shiver
from the future? She brings Ophelia
to life for every age, haunts
us today with uncertainties.

SPEAKING OF RIVERS

The river dappled air with moisture,
banished arid miles that hot October
hours before I reached Zambesi's shore
or came to face the fury of the Falls.
At my back were leaping, thieving monkeys
chattering like neophytes round a god;
their excitement echoed my emotion
as I stood by those almighty waters.

I could pray to the Ganges, would have liked
my brother's bones cast to that sacred Mother,
my father's ashes strewn on the Severn;
for rivers are deities to me
ever since the nailbourn
gave childhood summer days such magic
turning us to bridge–builders, beavers,
before it vanished for another span of years.

From a ferry approaching Quebec city
I launched my hopes on the St Lawrence
and, lately, relished wooded Rhone
sharing one stretch of its long journey.
I have watched Mersey host the world's
Tall Ships, shimmer for Britannia,
grace QE2. Back home I wade
in my estuary, offer daily orisons.

AUGUST IN GENEVA

Veiled Arabian women
choose shoes; dogs
jewel-collared
are lifted off trams;
buskers break into Mozart,
green turtles street dance,
pavements sprout bargains,
people buy, buy, buy.

No angels in St Peter's
no statue of Mary,
only Calvin's stiff-backed seat
in cathedral cool.
Below in the museum
teeth of Roman horses,
brooches, skulls
of Roman ladies.

Jet d'Eau towers
offers rainbows
to tourists, who
are unaware that
not long ago a young man
disdaining rope and pills
chose that mesmerising force
to blow him apart
fragmented
on to moored yachts,
the lake's waters.

A BATHE IN LAKE GENEVA

On this shore stood
Byron and Mary Shelley
he thinking of a certain prisoner
dungeoned across the lake,
her mind taken over
by that monstrous creation.
On summer nights they saw
lightning rip the sky in segments.

Beneath our feet hard stones
some slippery with weed
(which greenly rings my fingers).
With strident voices
a dance of ducks reminds
this is their territory;
yachts and dinghies sail past
with friendly waves,
windsurfers cut through
faces carved in concentration.

The eight year old sees a cruiser
returning to the city
and, swimming close together,
we fight against its wake
in exhilarated fear. Floating,
after waters quieten,
I watch jets over the Jura
coming in to land.

The younger child comes to me
laughing as she puppy-paddles
gulping water in excitement.
I, too, exult at being in these waters
fed by Alpine rivers, old
as earth itself,
new as dawning day.

THE INVITATION
(for Felicity)

"Why don't you come
in the water with me?"
my four year old visitor said
looking delightful
snow-balled in foam.

I had not shared a bath
since I was young
and my father danced naked
around the room
while two little girls
laughed and sang
knowing no more
about nakedness than
the sensuous slap
of waves on bare skin.

I hesitated, fearing
a child's cruel candour,
then took off my clothes
to sit in with her
blowing bubbles
tickling toes
sharing different stages
of femaleness.

TRUSTING THE RAINBOW

On my flat roof where no one could ask questions
nor point to my behaviour as eccentric,
I assembled wood to build an ark. I
have never even made a table, know nothing
of cubic lengths (which must now be in metres)
nor what tools suit different jobs. B & Q were helpful
and I watched Sailing Club members mend their boats.
Various complications, such as planning permission,
arose and neighbours twitched curtains, pointing skywards

when congregated outside. The vicar made a visit,
passed innuendos about my being over–zealous
and why should I be chosen when he was more appropriate?
Six hundred years of life must have given Noah skills
and God was quite specific about windows, doors and decks;
he had sons to help, while my daughters have left home.
I'll not say how long it took, but think in years not months,
while every day I wondered why, when no forecast
suggested floods, I was wasting money and time.

When a rainbow shone I remembered its promise
that earth should not again be ruined by water
which made my actions seem even more futile
and though I prayed for guidance no clouds ever parted,
no voice called "I am well pleased". Yet I went on building
and started to store food for animals and people.
One night TV showed clouds over the Atlantic
massed without a break and I thought "Now it will come"
so put provisions on board the finished boat.

But I woke to sunshine and, cursing my obsession,
dismissed the next night's storm. Even two weeks later,
when it was still raining, I did not see it as a sign;
not till neighbours came to see my work with hints
about a crew and weren't they the best people?
The vicar then suggested the boat should be christened
and could he come aboard? Certain friends I asked
would not leave their husbands and space was restricted.
My children all insisted there would be no flood.

Trusting that the rainbow meant the highest mountains
would this time be left alone, I hoped the girl in Europe
would drive up to the Alps. I wanted horses, cows,
sheep and pigs but could not afford them, expected
to rescue animals once I was afloat. The dog and cat
knew their quarters and I caught several pigeons.
Searching for the islands that decorate this estuary
all three were submerged and the opposing coastline
was slowly being swallowed as water levels rose.

Then strangers came bombarding and reporters
tried jummaring walls to reach my roof.
Televisions showed besieged shipyards, shops looted,
cars, heading for the hills, abandoned,
boats in suburban driveways surrounded by women
holding out children to be brought aboard, while crowds
pushed forward and crushed them underfoot.
I even saw two lovers lying near the water
waiting for death to bless their final consummation.

So I slept aboard now with radio and torches,
tools, First Aid kit and unopened charts.
One morning I was woken by unusual silence
found the boat floating on a strangely still sea.
I looked down into the water, down into a nightmare;
saw bubbles slowly rising from multi-storey buildings,
tree-tops, roofs, churches, streets and bridges.
An underworld of vengeance, no natural sea-bed,
and escaping from its thrall – tables, skateboards, cots.

Land I did not recognise sank in the distance
but scanning the horizon I managed to pick out
a pinnacle of rock not yet under water
where, with a cow beside him, a young man
cradled an infant and waved in desperate hope.
Once they were aboard, I began to trust that Someone
had a plan worked out. We picked up a pony,
a tortoise, fox and squirrel, exhausted robins
and wrens, a rabbit, two piglets and one lamb.

Old Noah had it easy, with his wife and sons' wives
and a much bigger boat, plus that dialogue with God
which I really envied. How we all fitted in
defies description, but the creatures understood
they must mix well if they were to survive while
Peter's small daughter proved a gentling influence.
We knew Noah's ordeal had lasted many months
so eked out stores, relied on catching fish
and made sure the cow was the best fed of all.

I longed to stand once more on steady ground,
reach my fingers into earth, lie on grass, climb
steep hills, smell primroses, hear beach music
(where waves would stay within their given place),
look over undulating views of wood and lane;
I even wanted to drive a car again,
enjoy shopping in a Sunday supermarket,
stand on a crowded escalator, go
to Heathrow to meet someone coming home.

I wanted all the despised, daily tasks.
In a desert I'd soon grow tired of sand
and seeing water all day everywhere much
lessened its attraction, though such abundance
helped to keep ourselves and the boat clean.
How we danced and sang when at last
clouds lifted and the rain ceased. Now
as we continued drifting round the globe
there were signposts in the blessed stars.

The sun shone too on our lonely craft
invisibly lifting layers of water. I worried
where and when we might land, hoped not to be
stranded high in Kamchatka or the Rockies.
I hoped it would not be long delayed
for space became more of a problem every day
since the pony, pigs and lamb had grown larger
and food was running out – except for fish
and never would I eat sardines again.

Playing with the radio one day, the child
heard voices, called me in excitement.
Then came what I'd long prayed to hear:
the distant crash of waves thrashing land,
the old eternal rhythm now re-born,
that partnership of earth and sea renewed.
The animals grew restive, sensing change;
we met danger in sudden juts of land
which Peter's memory of maps could often name.

He knew we were still in our own latitude,
a bonus I had not expected; I was afraid
we might drift to the Equator or one Pole
or hit that five-mile high mountain in Nepal.
Not that I could direct where we might land;
I could only keep us floating, keep us fed.
If the first flood served no purpose, this one
must have solved problems of over-population
and I dared not let my heart admit its pain.

Nor could I make plans for survival after landing
not knowing what resources there might be.
We had seen no other vessel on our voyage
but instructions must have been given
in other countries. I would not have been
the only modern Noah. There might be plagues
of frogs, locusts, flies or darkness yet to come.
Would our once computerised world ever return
not to target greed, this time, but good?

More land appeared every passing day.
I grew impatient to find harbour
and Peter several times restrained me,
made me wait till, almost unbelieving,
we saw contours familiar from long ago.
A few last drops of rain fell as we grounded
enough to arch a brilliant double rainbow
across the sky whose reflection
in still water bade us welcome.

FROM THE TATE GALLERY, LIVERPOOL

Whenever I find myself standing
in the Tate, my eyes
are always drawn to those arched windows
which either frame the view across the dock
– that great cathedral on the hill –
or focus on Mersey movement:
containers sailing out of port,
fat ferries disembarking at Pier Head,
heading for the other shore where cranes
at Birkenhead still reach for hope.

People say this renovation gave
ballet shoes to a mermaid;
but these buildings hold a past
full of portent, real as tomorrow.

Here I stand between
a city's two cathedrals
and its river.
Confront verities.

POEMS FROM THE LUCIEN FREUD EXHIBITION

I Double Portrait

A student on the gallery floor,
legs in lotus position,
stares absorbed at the canvas;
she seldom sees the whole
as people pass, pause,
interrupt her view.

Now she studies the white dog's
talkative eyes,
now the tassel of that green
dressing-gown,
now the large last toe.
One generous, revealed nipple
makes her own small breasts
rub against patterns
on a black T-shirt.

This is how he would like it.
If he slipped unheralded
into this room
he could join the crowd
unrecognised.

I come away with a sense
of reassurance
in my body, in my loving;
feel a giant
has gently held my hand
led me into sunlight.

II Two together

Above: a girl,
head resting on one hand,
stares with apprehensive eyes,
her chin touching the ribbed collar
of a jumper aggressively striped.
Beneath: a picture called
Rotted Puffin, where
only the beak is recognisable.

Both are from 1944
the year of Hitler's rockets,
Arnhem errors and a land
exhausted, still struggling
with a war now five years long.

Lucien was twenty-two, as
my brother would have been
were his remains not
already rotting in a jungle
continents away.

Others will make
different connections.

Juxtaposition jolts.

ON CONSTABLE'S *HAYWAIN*

I

The scene looks calm on canvas
conveys that noon hiatus when
the half—done day pauses,
but it would have been noisy enough
to distract Constable at his easel.

The dog must have been barking
and one man on the haywain
is arguing with his companion
or shouting at that mongrel.
Wheels, too, would have creaked
trundling past, and those ducks voiced
disapproval at being disturbed.
Horses, heavily harnessed,
blew bubbles as they drank,
relishing cool water after
labour in fields. Even that woman
washing clothes, if she felt easy
with the artist, could have been singing
out of tune or haranguing the men
for messing up her stream. A lark sang too,
perhaps, above the trees' rustling
and do those grey clouds threaten thunder
to ruin a year's hay harvest
and send a disgruntled painter
back to his studio?

II

Trite as place mats now, this picture
was a daring departure,
an outrageous depiction of nature
not then considered a fit subject;
worse, the figures were real people
doing ordinary daily jobs.
No artist seeking accolades
should waste his skill on such a composition.

But the hand that guided brush-strokes
was impelled by love of landscape,
its memories of childhood, courtship,
countryside known in intimate detail.
Calm comes from a heart at home.

HAIKU

Gift amaryllis
forgotten behind cupboards
punched through its carton.

GWEN JOHN

shy shadow

home–maker for cats
and nephews

aspiring saint

austere artist

consumed by passion
you revelled
naked
in wild seas

executed
in intensity
your canvasses

oases
of calm

renewal

AT DIEPPE'S HOSPICE
1st September 1939

When I put a crucifix in her hand
she managed to respond, seemed to understand
but who is the new patient on our ward?

> *Someone who came off the Paris train.*

Is she French or English? What's her name?

> *We have no idea; she has not said a word;*
> *she's too weak to be questioned, is half-starved*
> *and not a single person has inquired.*

She might have been trying to get home,
cross the Channel before war's declared.

> *She had no luggage, wears no wedding ring.*
> *For sure, that bed will be empty before long.*

*

Their destitute lived only a few hours,
none knew of her devoutness nor her art;
What would those nuns have felt had they but known
that the dying stranger was Gwen John?

THE LIVERPOOL CHRIST

The sculptor's life ended
when she completed this figure
which stands today above
the great west door
surveying streets, watching
the distant river
open to wider waters.

The hands touched me,
hanging down at his sides,
palms open,
offering no bribes.
Inside, in the transept,
that hay—cushioned infant,
in a sculpture of the Nativity,
lies defenceless,
palms open.

The reredos above the high altar
is dominated by Christ

hanging on the Cross, hands
wrenched wide
to receive the nails.

This artist understood nails,
knew pain,
signals acceptance.

RESURRECTION: THE REUNION
(after Stanley Spencer)

Gravestones tilt like deckchairs
as refugees from life, from death
lean back to survey the folk
they've lain beside for centuries,
greet loved ones left behind.

Children entwine arms,
a mother strokes the cheek
of her beloved daughter.
A girl waves in delight
at the one she came to meet.
Few smile, but the woman
with a Jane Eyre hair-style
looks with adoration
into her lover's eyes.

He wears checked trousers.
Most come clothed for today
though several are naked.
Only the living, allowed
here for this reunion
have shoes.

The picture holds no pain
only comfort, though seeing it
my heart calls certain names.
But resurrection can bring complications.
Spencer, playing Jehovah,
seems to have set a time limit.

No one tries to leave the graveyard,
no one wants to walk away.

REALITY
(International Red Cross Museum, Geneva)

Seven million cards stacked round me,
details of detainees during
this century's first long war.

I stand in a constructed cell
four metres square where seventeen
were held for ninety days.

I feel the weight of rubble that entombs me,
see stretcher—bearers coming
to lift me from the battlefield.

Starving, I receive a bowl of rice;
blinded, I am led to safety;
homeless, tent villages arise.

Yet I pulled the switch, controlled the gas,
I fixed your chains, denied you light,
made you dig your grave before I fired the gun.

And I am that man kneeling, broken,
as I am the woman giving comfort
broken, too, bowed by shock and sorrow.

CAMP BARBER AT TREBLINKA

My wife stood waiting in the queue
it was a shock to see her there.
Should I tell her what I knew?

Armed guards watched my movements too
I breathed a silent desperate prayer
as she stood waiting in the queue.

As, long ago, I used to do
I now prepared to cut her hair
should I tell her what I knew?

If I survive I will tell true
the cruelties we suffered here.
My wife stood waiting in the queue.

Gas would claim these people who
guessed not their fate, all unaware.
Should I tell them what I knew?

I whispered "Liebchen, I love you"
cropped her curls with tender care
watched her waiting in the queue
could not tell her what I knew.

REMEMBERING FEBRUARY 1991

There was nothing I could do about the war
but keep a candle burning in my room
hoping that at night it spoke to those
wounded, missing, distant and at risk;
begged Peace not to reject a world
at risk itself.

Candles offer intercessions
at a shrine, link
other conflicts, days when
people carried their own light
as they moved about a house,
climbed spiral stairs.

Igniting the wick each evening
seemed a futile act, yet it consoled
as if in breaking down the dark
in my small space I fought against
surrounding blackness, claimed
freedom to keep vigil.

I lit my candle night after night
and in the morning searched for rainbows.

INTERACTION

SARAH
My walk to the well after they had gone
was filled with unease. From the moment
he awoke, my husband acted strangely,
would not meet my eye nor explain
why he had to leave so early.
He ordered two young men to go
with him and told our son
he was needed too, though never
did he tell their destination.
They set off with a saddled donkey,
the lad, full of anticipation
of an outing with his father,
unable to control his happy grin,
the old face granite,
etched with pain.

ABRAHAM
Have I had to live these many years
to undergo such a test?
Was there no other way to give proof?
But this could not be questioned.
What the Lord had given
he now meant to take away.

Leaving home was bad enough
for Sarah sensed something wrong.
On the journey the boy
would keep talking, asking where
would we find the sacrificial lamb?
I had to tell him to be silent.

Part of me stood distant, witnessing
our progress as we drew near the place.
Numbly, I did what had to be done,
building an altar in preparation,
trying to delay the time
when my son would realise what was to come.

ISAAC
I helped him pile wood
for the fire and even after
he sent our men away
I did not feel afraid.
When he told me to mount the pyre
I thought it odd, for
we had not yet caught
any beast, but climbed
on top believing it a game.

With unexpected speed
he bound me where I lay
and pulled out from his coat
a knife whose sharpened blade
gleamed in the sun.
And I knew.

I could not see what made him
stay his hand, but he dropped
the knife before demanding
why I had not pointed out
the beast behind us trapped
in brambles. As flames consumed
the creature I had to turn away
and when my father suddenly
embraced me I turned away again.
Because I knew.

SARAH
They returned after a few days
but there was no joy in Isaac's eyes;
he had become adult in one leap,
looked at his father in uncertainty.
Now my nights are haunted
with dream on dream of fathers
who in obedience to custom
did not withhold the knife

and of one mother's torment
as she watched her son suffer
in sacrifice. Always when I wake
I run to make sure my son
is safe asleep in my home.

ON SEEING MILLAIS' *THE SCAPEGOAT*

He struggles to keep upright in that dire place
eyes red-wild with bewilderment
front feet encrusted, sunk.
Only his mouth looks vicious
as if to curse the cause of his distress.
His horns (shaped like an old ploughshare)

carry blood-red ribbons while
the sockets of a skull lie nearby.
Purpled hills rise in the distance
falling to a stretch of salted water.
His survival seems unlikely
words set in gold seal his doom.

Memories of sacrificing sons,
of captured lambs burnt on altars
still stain our hands and minds.
Goats, even in art, have a right to live.
This one's coat looks protective, warm.
I want to lead him home, bear my own sin.

NIGHT ROUTINE

Every night before he went to sleep
my father took off his watch
placed it by the three *Blackwoods*
on the chamber cupboard top
his side of the bed. Later
a mug of false teeth joined
the neat arrangement. Then,
pyjama–ed and bare–foot
he knelt to pray.

This ritual knocked down barriers
giving me the boy within the father.
I see him kneeling in Indian
bungalows, ship's cabin, hotel room
though his wound at Ypres
brought change for a time.

His bed, now mine, was an arena
for love and life and death:
three of us were born there
and it cradled him when dying.
Thus proper preparation was seemly
at the ending of each day before
he lay between the sheets,
mind quietened, reading till
his beloved came into his arms.

LAMENT FOR GRIEF
(for my father)

I miss my grief
as I once missed you;
I accept your death but
not grief dying too.

Ash like grief is
borne on the wind;
can its destination
be predetermined?

Has grief any say
where ash will blow,
does ash decide
where grief may go?

Ah, you would smile
being paired with grief
as you would weep
at my disbelief.

Ash nurtures earth,
grief grips love's hand;
your death, my sadness
weave one strand.

Ash is absorbed
grief has evolved
before the riddle
is ever solved.

POP

Nothing over years has taught
how to magic grief away. Touch
has no speech, is not educated,
yet brings understanding, as thoughts
from far away carve grooves across the sky.

Her name is lost
beneath detritus of decades
and she was not someone who
became a special friend though we
were both in our third year.

But that moment when Matron said
I must go and offer comfort
after news had come
of her father's sudden death
has never left me.

Not knowing what to say,
I hugged and rocked her, mingling
our tears, murmuring sounds to drown
– loud and shrill in the next room –
the soprano repeating and repeating:

"MY HEART BELONGS TO DADDY".

NEEDLEWORK

Once I embroidered standard roses
on a tray cloth for my mother
with crinolined ladies, their faces
behind brimmed bonnets,
lifting delicate fingers.
That pattern appealed because
tall Hybrid Teas and Floribunda
lined the path to our front door.

Blood was spilt but needlework then
could not be dodged, which meant
resentful thoughts were threaded
in my bird-print stitching.
At the end of term I presented
my work to her, not for any birthday
but as a toddler offers fistfuls
of wild flowers already wilted.

I never saw her use that cloth
nor knew if she was pleased.
Now when I see standard roses
in park or cottage garden
jabbing thorns remind
she is beyond my reach.

ABSENTEE

You will not be here
this Christmas
I must make sure
your empty chair
is set against the wall
not silent at the table
which you never were.

It will be the first time
since your birth
that, night-clad, we
have not opened gifts together,
you scrabbling beneath the tree
portioning them to each
member of the family.

Habits are hard to break;
no doubt I'll look
for you when I awake,
but then my heart will take
me rejoicing to the home
where you, my daughter,
cradle your new-born.

BEGINNINGS

A small head
to hold
stroke cheeks
examine each ear, toe
fist, finger—nail
search speedwell eyes
hear unfamiliar
crying.

In close contact
for months, we met
sixty minutes ago
when you began to learn
of air, food
caress.

Abandoning
that inland sea
you braved chasms
to discover
life.

We will journey now
with love our lantern.

OVERHEARD AT NURSERY SCHOOL

I would not have minded
snuggling up in hay
beside the fluffy donkey
that first Christmas Day.

I'd have liked the people
who came to see Him there
though some brought funny presents
like frankincense and myrrh.

His mum and dad loved Him.
I don't suppose He can
have often been a sad boy.
Mum's got another man.

Doesn't she ever miss me?
That's what I can't tell.
Someone said she's on the game
— I hope she plays it well.

I've got Dad. He loves me
but Mum has gone away.
I'd need no Christmas present
if she came back that day.

THE NASTURTIUM MARRIAGE

The service was mainly silence
which regulars used well.
With closed eyes one guest removed
her coat; its lining rustled.
An infant nuzzled his mother's breast.
A chair creaked. I could hear my heart beat.

A candle was lit, commitments made.
Silence. What would happen next?
Someone, propelled into speech,
likened that miracle with wine
to Paul Daniels on TV,
suggested Christ was in the room.

Recorder, flute and oboe spoke in joy
before a buffet in dazzling colour came,
nasturtiums sprinkling salads, encircling
bowls. One girl worried she might
unknowlingly have consumed caterpillars.
The room, no longer silent, buzzed with words.

Back home, the newly-married pair
opened presents, offered wine.
We sat outdoors, ringed by mountains.
At my side nasturtiums rampaged;
I watched caterpillars wrecking leaves,
picked and ate a flower.

Perhaps nasturtiums, like dog-roses,
negate plans they overhear.
When I returned one year later
nasturtiums were obliterated by nettles
and from inside the neglected cottage
came a haunted silence.

AN UNEXPECTED APPOINTMENT ON AUGUST 18TH

> "We were all very sorry on leaving to think of the
> possibility that we should never visit Grasmere Church
> again." (*Emilia Thornton's Journal, 1833*)

I went on impulse, not knowing
the significance of the date.
Nor had I read that journal
telling of your adventures
with young Matthew Arnold
when, after falling in the lake,
you made sure his clothes were dried
and his frail mother, who had recently
miscarried, not made anxious.

I did not expect to find the house
where the family stayed (the one-time home
of your father's friend Mr Wordsworth)
when you were just fifteen.
What made me stop beside a certain stone?
Was it where you hurt your ankle?
Who chose the pew in which I knelt?
Did you sit there each Sunday?

Crossing and criss-crossing the page
your girlish hand recorded
the three months' sojourn;
five days and nights spent
on the carriage journey from London
(visiting the "manufactory at Sheffield
and four ducal estates"), sketching
among rocks and streams,
"nutting" with your sisters,
your dislike of Hartley, Coleridge's son
and everyone's concern for Mr Wordsworth
suffering such pain from his eyes.

I did not know that you, young ancestor,
who died within two years of that holiday
also first saw Grasmere on August 18th.
Your longing to return must have nudged time.
Surely you sat beside me as I drove in sunshine.
You, Emilia, led me into lofty, misted realms.
What pattern have we completed or begun?

SPILT SALT

Impelled
by superstition
I draw the sign
across the salt spilt
on the café table.

Outlined in crystal
the crucifix dominates
food, cutlery, talk
as it has dominated man
since that curséd Friday.

Children
are told they
hammered hands to wood;
a lifetime's tears
will not be enough.

Guilt stays
like dirt under fingernails.
As a small insurance in dark places
my fingers form a cross.

RECOVERY IN THE CLWYDIANS

You'd come north for nourishment.
Turning right at Cilcain church,
left at the farm, my hands
lay lightly on the wheel
letting me drive by instinct
(along lanes where if two walked abreast
brambles would catch clothes)
hesitating only a moment
at crossroads on the moor.

At my side you talked
of the uncertain future
for a brain-wrecked son,
of the daughter who has too close
an acquaintanceship with death
and of the middle one, now seventeen,
rebellious, withdrawn.

Leaving the car to become
a dot of red in October sun,
we gambled with time and clouds,
yielded to impulse, forsook the track
to tread heather, scree,
till exhausted, exalted,
we lay laughing on the summit.

Westward, sunbeams pin-pointed Snowdon;
land to the east sought invisibility
and on the skyline question-marks
of hikers, weighed down by back-packs
and schedules. Outings often
fade from memory; these hours
will buttress and excite
long after our reluctant descent.

THE OUTSIDER

I never knew the man
whose death trawled us
that November day. His wife
(who'd died four days before)
lay waiting in the nearby
Friary graveyard.
I was merely chauffeur
enabling a blind friend
to bid a last farewell.

The parson at Pantasaph
spoke no comfort, kept
strictly to the service
for the dead. In the pew
the guide dog warmed my feet.

After the brief service
the sparse haul processed
to new-turned earth in wind
that moaned through glassless windows
of a neighbouring nunnery
and found weak places
in every person present.
As the coffin was lowered
the black labrador found
beneficial grasses.

I looked at the grey stones
(what have they not witnessed?)
of a building that still nurtures
those coming in retreat,
as it solaced Francis Thompson,
and hoped this unknown man
might also find peace here.

But at the gathering later
I found shreds of untied ends.

FINDING BILLY BUTTON

Not a place for laughter this
where Beverley aged only two
lies close to John Stephen who
did not live long enough to walk.
No, it is not a place for laughter.

Sunlight polishes the red of roses,
black sheen of funeral cars.
On newly-dug earth sits a teddy bear
of white chrysanthemums
and raw pain claws away my calm.

This place insists I cannot count
on my tomorrow, nor the tomorrows
of my children. Here death shows
no pity, choosing young Dawn
at fourteen, Robert – thirty-nine.

No, this is no place for laughter
yet when I find the headstone
of *mourned and beloved Billy Button*
he manages to make me smile
and walk my grief back to the busy road.

UNIDENTIFIED BODY ON DUNES

One tear trickled down her face
Surely the dead cannot cry?
Who was she in that dreaded place
One tear trickling down her face?
Now the pathologist must trace
When she'd died and decipher why
One tear trickled down her face
Surely the dead cannot cry?

OUT OF DARKNESS

The saddler at Coupvray,
welcomed his son
into a three year-old's paradise.
Small hands explored the workshop,
appreciating tools.

No one else was present
no one saw what happened
in the year Napoleon
(taking the best doctors)
began his Russian march.
The boy poked an awl in one eye
and neither herbs nor plasters
could save his sight.

Adult hands turned into tools;
fingers prized an awl again
to punch a six-dot code
known now by his name. But
they fell to immobility
forty years from boyhood
stilled by tuberculosis,
carried home by horse-cart
buried in a churchyard
undisturbed for a century.

The body then was lifted
and borne in procession
to the Pantheon.
Coupvray rejoiced to see its son
accorded recognition,
but felt bereft without him,
so his hands were severed
brought to that empty grave
in a concrete casket.

Look not for him in Paris.
Go to his village to salute,
venerate those hands.

LIVESTOCK SALE

I watched a man spray blue crosses
on sandpaper backs of pigs
as they pushed snouts through bars
against my hand. He marked them
for collection by the abattoir.

But I could not look at colts
no one was prepared to take
for winter grazing. Bids
for these came only
from back rows and all
understood their destination.

Disembodied voices cried bargains;
trees that day were phantoms,
the market shrouded in fog
as if surrounding fields, where those foals
first tried their Lowry legs,
could not bear to see them driven away.

When the auctioneer, reluctant
to bring his gavel down on a butcher's bid
for a school—girl's pony, persuaded
a farmer to take it for a fair price,
a veiled sun broke through.

CONFRONTED BY PEACOCKS
(for Kit)

Six peacocks and a hen
parade across my pathway,
perch silhoutted at night
in an oak's high branches;
ostracised by the rest
one roosts in a ruined oast.
Since these birds prefer
a harem each, I wonder why
this muster boasts but one bride.

In his monastery garden
Brother Sebastian mourns
those five victims, condemns
the cocks who flew away
to escape the fox, praises
single-minded hens
for staying on their nests.

Defying the fox of superstition,
during the moult,
families nearby seek
Chaucer's "angel" feathers
to decorate their halls.
They know peacocks once
were favoured by a goddess
and hope, perhaps,
for divine protection.

Meeting peacocks now
for good or evil
I too feel touched by gods.

ON ROMNEY MARSH

weeping willow
water streamers
slant   trail
shelter swathes
of chiffon
pierced by flint eyes
a disembodied
fold

waves' sigh
shingle sweeping
voices muffled
smugglers   cognac
slam of shutter
victims cower
knives   guns
gold

willow whisper
swaying lanterns
owl screech
hands scrabble
rough justice
in bog swallow
choked sobs   bubbles
cease

today
cloud-shadows
dapple dykes
Martello towers
flit over flocks
children play
catkins dance
in peace

PAST PERFECT

Six poplars and an oast-house
stood on the sky-line above
our farm's sloping fields.
When we ran to the village
past the white Norman church
this horizon reassured.
Wherever we might walk
home checked on our welfare.

Post-mistress and butcher,
blacksmith and school-teacher
knew where we came from,
knew that hill. When hay-making
we could gaze at wooded Kent
stretched below, see
which fields burgeoned
with hops, which orchards
boasted White Heart cherries,
where secret lanes led, where
the nailbourne flooded a road.

I carry this landscape
internally. It is my country,
stays intact within my heart.
But it is cobweb threatened,
spidered by road and railway
and the sprawl of parasites
spewing from that tube
beneath the sea.

LESSONS FROM AN ORCHARD

Long weeks ago I brought this apple home,
a ripe and shining present from a friend.

It rested on the table fresh and green;
white rings today decorate brown skin.

Since there is no obvious sign of rot
even now I cannot throw it out.

Light as locks of hair when I pick it up
the under side is like a contoured map,

ridges and gulleys mark a dark terrain;
the whole has shrunk to less than half its size.

Closely guarded on my study shelf
it brings to mind Oscar's masterpiece.

How much am I in the decomposing fruit?
Has any part, a pip perhaps, stayed good?

I wonder why those rings have not coalesced
and need to know what will happen next.

It has taught me much, informing that
Schiller needed smell of apples to write,

kept them rotting in a drawer in his room.
This apple has for me become an icon.

GOODNIGHT-AND-GOODMORNING-AND-DON'T-FORGET-WHITE-RABBITS-IN-SIXTY-SECONDS
(for Terry, Radio DJ)

They lolloped in at once
not waiting until midnight
took me by both hands
bounded through the house
out into the garden
where beneath a white-faced moon
they danced around me
as beams of silver light
partnered them with shadows.

Two hares emerged
from behind the rhododendron.
They bowed stiffly in reproof
as if to ask had I forgotten
that we were told as children
to say "Rabbits and Hares"
the moment we awoke
on the first of each new month;
there was an extra custom too
of walking backwards down the stairs.

When I acknowledged their salute
and affirmed their long tradition
the pair were welcomed in the circle.
Then the ground began to quiver
as the dance grew ever faster
till the figures fused together
and suddenly were gone.

In silence I walked up to bed
backwards and alone.